Everyday and Prophet